Incognegro

D.S. MARRIOTT was born in Nottingham 1963 of Jamaican parentage and was educated at the University of Sussex. He has taught there and currently teaches at the University of California, Santa Cruz. He has written many articles on poetics and is the author of *On Black Men* published 2000 by the University Presses of Edinburgh, and Columbia, New York; and *Haunted Life* published 2006 by the University Press of Rutgers, New Jersey. *Incognegro* is his first book of poetry.

Incognegro

D.S. MARRIOTT

SALT

CAMBRIDGE

PUBLISHED BY SALT PUBLISHING
PO Box 937, Great Wilbraham, Cambridge PDO CB1 5JX United Kingdom

© D.S. Marriott, 2006

The right of D.S. Marriott to be identified as the
author of this work has been asserted by him in accordance
with Section 77 of the Copyright, Designs and Patents Act 1988.

First published 2006

Printed and bound in the United Kingdom by Lightning Source

Typeset in Swift 9.5 / 13

ISBN-13 978 1 84771 261 8 paperback
ISBN-10 1 84771 261 3 paperback

SP

1 3 5 7 9 8 6 4 2

for Andrew Crozier

Contents

Acknowledgments

Acknowledgement is made to the following publications, in which some of the poems in this book appeared originally: *Angel Exhaust*; *Callaloo*; *The Capilano Review*; *Exact Change Yearbook*; *Folded Sheets*; *Fragmente*; *Grille*; *Hambone*; *Jacket*; *Lamb*; *Poetical Histories*; *Scarlet*; *Talisman*; *Ten British Poets*; *Tyonyi*; and *West Coast Line*. A number of poems were also published in chapbooks by the following presses: Equipage (*Lative*); Prest Roots Press (*Airs & Ligatures*); Barque Press (*Dogma*). The versions here preserved are, however, somewhat different and are final.

Lative

The Ghost of Averages

1

hard work,
      hard even for a nigga, but not you.
The French grammar,
      lies open on a table
smeared with grease, oil, —
      unfettered by the chains
 opening the mind begins its flight
and maybe, . . .
      who knows. . . .
the harvested cornfields are green, once again,
    a home for what can be reclaimed
            rather than loss, or delusion,
derided by you, Booker,
      as proof the ancient memories lie unredeemed.

2

There is hard work
        in the school yard.
I am Kunte Kinte on the hill,
the stars torn from the rolling dusk,
        I sit side by side
with the dark, the unwelcome brown.
Re-read says my father,
        the coal dust lining his eyes
the focus
        for the reprieve of time, the art of discovery,
                for the receipts
of less gnarled hands and feet.
        He used to call me 'dee',
reminders, too, of how missed letters
        are often the most permanent of things
when the tin can spills
onto the oilcloth near the unopened book
and he takes deep breaths
on his knees
        reading the seams of coal for 'this is not-me'.

3

I wrote his funeral program in *Word*.
    If one day,
    life rains on you
    a similar dereliction and collapse,
        read that French grammar.
And the boy,
pitied for the ever patient, worn-out binding,
    the loneliness and levels of neglect,
gives tithes against his will:
    remember what is valued, the price it gives.
The privilege is reserved for us—
    Each letter blackened
because a wish to live is deeper
than seams to be mined,
        or eyes darkened by dust.

Someone Killed Them

The sadness fits the sudden and violent end —
      or is it just the longing to know what happened?

You wake up,
Where are you?
You can't get used to being dead,
      your body hanging from the railings
      not far from home.
Who's that beside you?
Hanging with an electric flex round his neck — its your uncle.
You haunt the town of Wellington, the brick walls and parked cars.
Your deaths seem weirdly believable.
What day is it?
Millennium New Year's Eve.
You were safe until 11.55 p.m.
Then you walked through the pub door . . . .
      Sinead sits waiting for you at the Elephant & Castle. She still is.

Orange & Green

Come, Caecilie, come.
We need to carry this thing forward,
get back, go beyond,
as we sit, talking,
drinking coffee,
riding in cars & trying not to remember
the old familiar me, the precious one.

                    Sometimes
it's just the fading; taste
the assignment of what lingers, what is.
Do you miss all that? Do you miss 50s TV?
                    The world inside our heads
keeps us going past the orange stripes of sunset
beyond the green trees, till we stop. The black dog
hams it up as if he were a wolf
and not the old urbanite he is!

The eye of the TV burns on the dark yellow walls,
a little yeast, for the romance of memory,
never revealing, ever concealing, the wound that matters:
as we live by the heart,
lit by our thoughts, sure of welcome,
whispering behind the lips we kiss.

The 'Secret' of this Form Itself

it begins at the border
                    intimate as skin
searching for a sentimental foreignness or fusion
        all these restless voices
reflected in the antiplace
          where we enjoy the status of victims
the disease and compensation
        tricks of fate?

when we stepped off the boat
        the tide, the long imperial gain,
extended to all colonies,
debased by the raw stink,
the world retched in the advocacy, we were the script—

what secret
           emerges from these idylls of nations, at the mercy of ringworm gods
                                  arteries open
                    wide to the
                          purity of island stories—
do we love the obsession,
        this way of being a blocked wall
screening out more desolate places?

as when wading through a warm stinking mess to meet my father,
lightscreens in the back of my cropped skull,
a whirlpool of shapeless heads screaming in the darkness
        I want to let go—but cannot
there is no consolation, the opaque derision
anonymous, racially compelled

I didn't know air could burst into white flame
                    or that the weak,
dying on an outlying island, could sing useless lieder of queens and empire

I would love to lock the door
                    ease the flood
fresh on last night's storm
safe,
this landed world a dream
edifice of scaffolds

what emerges is an unmistakable symmetry
                    driving their buses
                    their trains, wiping away
all the blood and foulness of their arses,
making tea with sugar seeing
                    the chains and mutilations
                    done by cultured men
framed for posterity
                    on the horizon of an idea

pressing their way
into the long sweet paralysis
of so many years lost, wandering
                    adrift in memory

this space that is open to us could so easily be lost
          we have neither the books nor the city
only the many reflections of polished floors and corridors
          a surfeit of forgotten traces without rank or honour

I didn't know the depths of these unspoken things,
                              or why I had to wait until 1963
to sound them out in the parade of a new age
watching Adidas shop-windows and gold chains
                    the repeated denials
along the way drifting back to the real.

For Invisible Black Vampyres

For invisible black vampyres, unseen in the shining refuges of day
the stake of my nigger-death. These spook-bearing wraiths,
passing through shadows, through stairs
toward swampwater mists and virgin forests, the fetishes and threats,
which move me, bury me,
as you float toward me under miraculous suns in chains,
unburied, undead
among black effusions and evil spells
among white images dining on catatonic nigger-dolls
as we fade with the small hours, return with the dark night,
formidable friends
black hearts become great clefts of flesh
when penetrated by your rich red blood.

Because you are blackblack umthakathi,
black vampyres, fed on beasts on hope on our unshadowed skin,
where vaults, by undivine right
by immemorial natures, embrace you,
know you are the horn and the bone, the locust and the drought,
from you come storms and hunger
an anaemia of sense, in you the invisible terror
of your vanishing, save us by feeding long and well.
We have no magical poisons and yet the cities stare at us
and the thing that really burns
that sucks out the last breath
is not the unavoidable deadness going crazy and unloved
crazy because unloved,

but the numerous pieties of violence,
all-white, all-seeing,
fatal and dark even in death.

You will learn again the simplest things last,
of fauna and of herb, of the perfect whiteness bringing pain and death,
if you remember how to receive them on the first
rising, if you remember that each black image
is itself a grave. Don't be frightened of fresh wounds
the babies or the brides, you know they will make
dust of our lives.
Be merciless on the high mountain paths
above the villages and cornfields, at the archway and threshold,
memorial as a bourne that binds us to the throat of freedoms past.
For you inherit the shadow totems of insolent nihilismus,
of the too much black leather beret and the too much black leather cape.

By virtue of our old sufferings of our old laments
by way of a solecism in this beautiful black blood,
you appear, black vampyre; and you are the most soulful of us all
with all these white-black deliria exploding around you
and seduce us, in spite of ourselves,
scavenging on shelters and badness and dopescreens for the hood.

Ice-cold

1

when the ice hardens in the soul
                    who is not chilled by it?
I mean when the rich brown is ashen and the blood is stopped cold,
and wigga thomas' crazy ass
                              is mind-whipped
        by the waves, the ice, forming black crystals.
The ice hardens in the soul:
but life is a continual burning,
        so much so and to such a degree
that the pain is unrelieving, unsolaced,
too hot or too cold,
this numb intensity like a furnace in winter,
or else an X
        seen burning throughout the night—
              the fate earned in sight of the middle passage,
      when snow falling
    is the most serene, terrible feeling of deadness.
I mean, ice-cold when the only open country
        is the life left behind, no longer substantial—
        and not in limbo, either,
but the entropy that remains when sky and night fall away,
    and all life is the work of this slow freezing. . . .

2

Black men unloaded and packed into prisons,
  colder, much, than the iron bars holding them,
the mind nothing but winter,
  given fresh ice to pack the emotions:
    I see that life, my own life,
burning like blocks of ice in the approaching dusk.
Talk to any one of them and they will tell you,
  that iciness can last years before the thaw begins.

3

Let's say frozen in familiar remoteness
    the earth, colder now,
    is just one hard, commercial block
of ice, refrigerated, ready to go—
    blended in the whiteness
and frozen quickly by its own descent
in the icy depths of space—
then, with an eloquence that thaws, or melts,
the good that remains, encased in ice, is pitch-black:
    imagine the surprise
  as the earth goes skimming over the arc:
    would E.T. have come here first,
or would he have changed the order of visits—
self-standing
    this colder than a motherfucka
                star
  so extra and on edge:
inside the glacial flow of meltwater traffic,
  moving from one icy mound to another,
we ask once again:
    would a nigga from outta space
see this as a proud quality of becoming,
or would he say
    I ain't freezing my black ass off here?

Bridge

laws of the city for nothing gets lost,
the unwritten laws of the dead for the dead, —

I feel old here, defeated,
lean, unshaven, sick and limp,

surprised at the flesh sagging,
reacquainted with my indifference to sex:

too old to change, too young to love anybody but myself—
listen, then, to my story:

of how the streets are narrower, the buildings smaller,
than remembered; of how a tree in a park was rescued

from the developers of mainland classical culture.
Who are they, standing around doing nothing?

Ten years of my life lost to the weight of things,
the constant reversals, the humbling taste of glory,

and think of the rooms, the tiny shared rooms where family gathered,
a loss barely glanced at in the light of day.

The Steerage

Now the air is thought as the void,
mingled with hail and the dark waves, no less,
perhaps, than the remaining fall of snow.

The whole is full of light and obscure night
together, both equal, since neither is for sake
of courtesy, and neither is for the sake of snow.

I do not see the sense of rare privilege
putting heroism into words of arbitrary redoubt
when we go forward so slowly, walking alone
and in the dark, circumspect lest we fall.

The waters upholding us are a shining brightness,
a whiteness in the cold, when, without yielding,
what is not lost to us comes so seemingly close
as to shimmer variably into beached form.

I have known the shearwaters, gulls and tern
to be diurnally insured, a gross mean in rains
which should have convinced me even then
that the hardnesses were bound linearly,
carrying the lower bounds to the nesting wilds,
depleting as the frozen waters drew close.

But the plundered completions under affine obliquities,
plundered to earth and turning to sea, were abiotic,
or nonliving, fittingly disposed as a geodesic mean.

And we are born to it, at each
successive level, going towards the proper
distances of stars but surpassing all
we do by a natural love. The visible
energies are as balances in the lists
and still we have no names for the cosmic colds,
knowing each day to be a signed and prevenient
auxiliary, distributed unevenly over the world.

Even when the cold is deepest and hurt grips
aloof in broadest day, each resistive night
has only one name, reflected in our signs; and
in our journeys we drive past to the shortest day.

And always we are known in the midst,
past the animals trembling in the open stances,
and onto a verge without plea; faring over the way
that is like shearwaters in the whiteness that falls,
our regress without primacy on the leeward sea.

As an angel once led Tobias, when, on feet
of charity never swerving, he saw
the nearness of what is uttered and what is,
the different as commodity in the sight of things
and the pain that was; so also do we see
the long night of irreducible being
over an endless sea, in the loss that knows.

The Going Tides

As we turn without doubting
through waters of the knowing world,
remembering the sum of your dying
and all my surer years; the

squalling clouds disable us,
thought the genoa sails furl clear.
Imagine the dark spectacle
of such readiness gathered in the lees;

the infused sight of cloud
merged with moments of despair,
as we turn to grace and the grace seen:
formerly held to being, and ease of keel.

And always to have suffered
that which you alone can give;
the blinding and threshold so true
to starboard the dark skies

seemed imperious in the water's descent.
Inseparable and without reason.
The oars were gifts but sufficed
nothing. Love to us a certainty

of the sails having filled.
Now you are going, and the great
pouring forth billows out the will.
On the tiller the heart's water;

and the kind seas holding all now dead.

The Dream, Called Lubek

Now blacks, in the hold, working.
The harbours, overhung by mist. The canvas,
overseen by frost and rain.
The freest sea rides in to port. The air
refreshes ladies out on afternoon strolls, out for gain.

Perhaps the snow cleaves them,
their tongues passwords or gifts
concealed in dreams or memory of stars, else handed names
like coughs to sweeten the white acid-salt.
I am one of them like a glass in the sun.

As on a dark sea where no other is,
desolate in the screen never landing in desire;
wishes in with the tide, washed-up and tiered,
turning the sails on to dark horizons, on to dark rock;
seas of submergence
in which there is no place, no access,
cast out upon forgetfulness with no vessel,
pursued in the breakage of the wake.

To be myself inside the witness
where memory falls in remembrance
like a deluge; neither tribunal, nor excuses,
as I floated on the mirroring and a sail drew near,
nor withdrawal as the days and years become air and salt.

To be myself inside the witness,
witnessing the lost one never coming back,
all the recriminations and betrayals and disappointed lists,
as if in my thoughts there was a darkness,
without finitude or fascination,
which exists, has no burial, it resumes
neatly inside myself like an open grave.

To be adrift inside the reigning green,
deep in the midst and unfathomable seas,
overboard in the depths of each shining reflection
so false they return unnamed; a past never present,
down below a cloudless dark on the edges of waves.

On a road that is no road, the air dark with persistence:
the never-found names, appear. We receive
their iridescence in the form of human sewers and ashes.
We ensure their kenning through loss and sacrifice.

Knowing that the sacred cannot be housed here
after the silences of so many years, after the weaknesses of our disunity.
We return to what is lived in the barrenness
of what is desecrated, for tragedy is never enough
for what remains of us, nor what is lost the greener.

〜

In the morning a heavy rain and wind came on.
Free as air
that scours from across the sea.
The last sheared tides as the lash speaks through
    what occurs, what cannot, what remains.

Bolo's Last Voyage

Neither cut memories, nor chrome, nor brass,
nor the booksellers'
commercial equipage, treating words as old rope
in shingles and silt of the sea,
but a storm-wind from the open heavens,
holds the mind's destinies
to the limitless seas,
turning the sails
onto dark horizons,
the raging swells of sea.

Shot

As the snow came down, star-tipped, our hopes fell with it;
struck and gone. It's a hindrance to living.
This, the first week of June
as the brothers are falling
one by one
into the withdrawal symptoms of early summer.
Let's shoo away the disease, set it down,
unfurl the sheaves of the word 'suffer'.
Gunshots bring news of something we know and want no part of,
news time surges in between the one that keeps the world going,
the steep, slippery sidewalks of deferral
blown deep inside us
shut up behind the doors, gone before the shot interrupts it.
It's a matter of time and causes no surprise—it's the weather,
it causes us to run backwards, back from any ray of light,
back to the wilderness in whose freakish and unspeakable midst,—
the noise does not tend towards consolation—
darkskinned and shirtless
stranded in drifts of snow,
the sharp-tongued words of black angels:
fathomless the thrust, the barrens.
We have been waiting around all night for it
(a freer and more dangerous bloom)
stretching out on the avenues,
seductive, exact, diving the pearl sap
and excrement of all the spurted blood they pass through:
the whiff of fulfilled dreams

as midmorning ice and smog surges up on promises never meant to be kept.

Snow-stars drift away in ashes,
heat eyelashes down on black divas—their promises—
and what does it matter anyway
eyes wide and strong, or weak, sick, cold, castrated?
Time darkens against the breakwaters
as shattered bodies pile up, swelling in the stench and heat,
the rumble of mourning and loss
pulsing through dark, endangered bodies, the eyes and ears,
needle veins and breasts—
the only expectancy: dying to live because so much easier than love.

~

We could sleep together again but we won't,
colours become blue, a chaos of the polestar and our darksightedness;
this blindness our death, dead, the precise click in the lock;
a sign from the skies come down like a pound of greyish-white ashes.
We live it, black every night and white in the morning,
alive like a stretch of light and beachsand after a dangerous trip at sea.
It ain't teached us yet,
even though as homeboys we are a great and heavy thing;
an horizon of fear
under the cross and mack and whore's crackpipe tongue,

the return of bonfires in snow falling. The air prone to vanishing.

We want the rites of life
like roots of downward sap dark with nightsweats,
scorched, in turn, by snow by suns,
but the summer disfigures and marks us way too much,
and night, desired, deliverer, ain't nothing but the real thing.

Ashlands

Ash, the unfinished tides. The
　arch of sovereigns. Saved

we broached a rod of wood;
　sliding contracts in a composed

flood, the vertices, the alter.
　Unfounded vowel in a passage-

grave. Half-cells burnish, subdue
　my face for shame. Thetical advent

roasting a heart punished for a
　crime.

Spears rest, execute & chronicle.
　Wide lands, flat stones. Owing

to the resistance of the spark gap
　desolate place by the shore.

Caiques flow on the tides. Fining
　preserved narrative, the staggering

remand of hope. Forms of salt dampen.
　Cairns ribbed by sunlight. The

youngest son wrestles with Cain &
　pulsars sense in succession. Cliffs,

desolate moors. Renowned champions
    defrayed the cost, choked the

nucleus of the seed. Grettir sick
    at heart in a bottomless deep.

Old and new endure extremities of
    an arc. Chord the sharing place

with cartilage, plexus. Parching
    opifex. Winter trees darkening

the water. In many ways his malice
    is a hard kind to be eaten raw.

Thermal flows & honour's linear
    resistance the moral sense

attuned to kings; the restless name.

Incognegro

Back-a-yard is wey de fuss is,
and the moon bright in the scuffed mirror.
Me nuh see wha a gwan,
but the glass reflects what is real and what is not.

Dem sey dem feel involve
even though pity is missing from the gaze,
a lapse, a density, as the bizzies armlock him,
so him put up nuh fuss, an dem candemn im to damnashan—

the thought of calling her mobile
for our own peace of mind, only.
Wi look like wi headin back to de grave,
but the soul is so unlikely a captive,

dem nieda see nor do dem feel
the smoke above the ash trees, the banks of fog,
de time incognegro an nat a dyam ting
but silence at the other end of the line.

Im sit wid us in the dark, de man nuh respec us,
the fault is in the cold night air,
in the grim, deep and unsettling form of the mirror.
Di pathos an disenchantment, undastan, lass beyan rekonin.

Du Bois in Berlin

As on a cold day in early spring
the tramways glisten and birds descend on gaping caverns:
shitty, leaden, Byzantine. And I dance
with Dora, who is strawblond struck by the sun, —
no longer on the outside of the world, looking in.

We mix words like coffee and milk:
freiheit, stammheid, Tannhauser. 'Gleich,' she said.
And yet there is a sickness inside me, so dark—
my will—it falters—my pen smeared with ink.
I have chosen exile—it is not an easy art to master; it is no worse than death.
For where life has once been, love is ruined.

In Friedrichstraße, knocking on closed doors,
warmed by the pleasures of the arcades
                    wandering at night
after Trietschke's lectures under the vaulted ceiling. And the hush
as old words are made new again. As if each *Wort*
          were signed in blood, and rising above it,
an angel pushing back white mounds of garbage.

In this house I, too, revel in a sacrifice to history.
The landlord sits in the corner reading Goethe.
He listens when I talk: *dichterisch*, when history
unfolds like the wadded bills in his pocket.
Even here, dark and cold, my tattered soul is bliss.

The way moonlight falls in the first-floor window
and the air glows warmly, what can I do . . . the world is evanescent.
It should have been a warning to me; it wasn't.
The eye of darkness floats over the pyramid,
this is how I must live, all memories missing . . .

'Mihi quaestio factus sum,
            et ipse est languor meus':
today the colours matter as do the sublimes
passing through the cathexia filling my room,
as people pour out into the streets from work,
and time grows darker on the wet black branches.

To feel such longing alive without knowing it
— the grandeur a long list of hopelessness —
when the writing down of names
and the dark season closing in,
makes the world so beautiful I am aching.

'Die Mulattin ein sind niedrig! Sie fuhlen sich niedrig':
the voice is high and accelerating, each word clad in spurs,
each theatre of thought a bulwark by the sea
fighting the breakwaters and the dark night gathering.
And this is good, a true thing. The lights go out by the canal . . .

warships on the Spree, their flags flailing in the wind,
passing from port to port,
                            boatloads of shit in full regalia:
gray clouds encircle them, as do endless crowds—
I hear the cannons go off and am thrilled by the spectacle.

On the stairway I thought of Dora.
We listened to music at Eisenach, sang Wagner.
No end. No end. No end.
Out of step with my youth and the force of desiring
as our two bodies touched, and our two minds, too:
and yes—nothing more—but the faultless surrounding with two people in it,
        borne on the tide, lost in the mist,
                    briefly intimate in the great dark danger.

This morning in the courtyard under a rainy sky,
I felt doomed in ways I do not wish to name.
Whatever the world really is, I want time:
to wear the decade like a diadem until too heavy to lift,
and the great strife echoes in grief-blackened veils.

The Consolation

The smoke from a skywriting plane spells $d\ldots d\ldots$
Time moves slowly in the coolness of the room —
no rain for three years, exodus on the warm, humid plain where sleeping apart
   from strangers
                    stops the trembling
of her tired limbs,
         her heart great-girthed and stained,
  as doctors disappear from the ritual
        weathered and gray, courtly and thoughtful:
        where the smell of formica tables, trolleys, antiseptics,
reflect nothing but the mire. I touch the outerpart of her flesh. The animals
   look like old people
               without mouths or skin,
         as the skywriter's smoke drifts to $y\ldots p\ldots$
the way a foetus braids memory for the private life of a name:
         and we are saved by the poisoned air drunk
spewing pendular arcs in the sky our fate exemplary.

The way we are suddenly fearful to look back on deck, desolation
   the work of leaving, because we are born that way:
and clouds of rain
               begin to gather in the heavens
        as she walks backwards in the corridor because lost —
           where sleeping apart she chokes on the severed tongue $e\ldots a$
     my mother's eyes dimmed by the medications,
and I am part of this moment as the plane drifts overhead
   unerring as a wish returning from the land of the dead.

And there is nothing but the merest sign
of language
      as the animals close their eyes shocked by the movements
        of their own limbs.

I know that the sun is rising over the docks
  as we haul these griefs ashore
held aloft above tides of excrement, the towers and chimneys—
  the patient future of human desires
a symbol, revealing nothing but catastrophe and flood,
   the emptiness of all household gods, nailed to the prow
        as a priest utters certain phrases.
Does it matter that each echo
         is a symbol less innocent than assent,
submerged by fitful breathing
        carrying us to the land of the dead,
where the sounds are glorious as dark waters rush in
to mingle with her departing wish,
       the gurgling of the condemned,
as rain splashes down on the surging swell
and the heart-shaped language of my mother,
        overshadowed by dark circles of pain
and the life lost to a box of ashes scattered at sea.

My Secret Life

S. "Mother, you can never mark it, this
    open bronze door, pitched lid, until
    the elegy of heaven caught you, and
    water severed both your long arms."

M. "My son, your pale eyes warm the cobblestones
    near the tramlines; remembrance is
    a cold utopia of the nut-tree smell
    and moistened earth. Look how well the
    small birds glow, their plumage dream,
    whilst eating the scattered seeds."

                        ∽

    The binding line is a golden era
    as the stones tremble with death.
    To gaze at a face so sadly,
    inhaling dust because time is ageless;
    the days, weeks, months
    washed and shaved every day, —
    a sort of bloom the world scorns.
    To thirst alone in the small house
    her belongings in a shopping cart
    (Jim Reeves or was it Val Doonican?)
    a rosary to call us forth, fugued, a psalm,
    because light is possible when living in the dark,
    and memorabilia the end when reached. That I
    am troubled so burns the leaves
    of memory; the we that scatter
    so in the years' untroubled winds.

We walk together in the garden until she drifts away . . .
she smiles at every face except mine—
I don't know why.

A Disputation on Pentecost

1

Max, I am leaving today. Don't forget me.
Outside, everybody's shouting:
and the dreams, winds, streams or snows —
first-created harmonies of the dead,
as I turn to you once more, and vaunt the good way;
for the possessive day quickens me, and calls
the living and the dead from paradises and pleasances,
to suffer again the good-for-nothing death.

Beyond these caught fires lie our souls, and approach
with swords and staves, dreams and obsessions,
unaltered across the folded range; how clear
this theft is out of the mouths of the shining Lords, spent
on the bare hills, broken to shivers,
commending waysides of some remembered ceremony;
and how their eagled watching is so piercing
amid the ferns and grasses: this abutting folds to perfection,

and glorifies the dead on stony wastelands,
whose seven spirits are seven stars in the night sky,
and whose remains defile the roots, blacken the waters,
their voices heard in the greater depths,
soiling the ear, awaiting the future to unveil their glory:
I realise this is a second death,
when pain burns in the marrow, and the names
enthrone torment and desolation.

When the brimming basin overruns,
vinegar and gall is the parched way up ahead;
the eaten flesh spewed onto spilling water,
which is the second death:
but natural government has no ordained end,
the roosting hawk rests on the towers—
is married to the concord, sinew and flesh—
and we too govern this horde within a chaos of nets.

I don't care—elect violence is the pity;
neither brightness raining down on ash and stone
nor the glowing air blinding the stare,
maunder by unnerved suffering; the newer towers
are a mosaic for a hawk hovering;
brought to memory as blind assurance—
red innocence on high green.

Unequal laws compel the fashioning—
on the glacial heartlands, the transience and miracles
reach the mind's permafrost, inland ice,
equal the shining wings in fiery clouds,
with all the lives condemned to mortmain's dominion,
and all the leaves foliage to our fires: Max,
the lawgivers say cold in the stadiums.

And what if the pleasances bind the dead
sow tares upon a lion's blood, and disagreement
and strife kneel down before a *complementall* heaven
touched by the purging violence of the fire;
are these just ligatures for the rank infested blood
spilling on incised tongues,
to hinge our passion with our guidance?

Does the secure way shine as light over water?
the unwilled pilgrimage of the poorer dead,
and other quests, give light to suffering
like marks in new snow in late winter;
which is the second life barred from mercy:
Max, here is no consummation, there no return,
we are in exile from the pity,
in utter isolation from the flesh of our fathers' loves.

2

Max, remember me when the dark rain falls . . .
When the tower is a shield against inundation,
upwelled by labour from the world as known.
In such immobility we weigh upon our darknesses,
having neither site nor place; in the prefecture
desire once removed, reflected in the intenser sun,
ministering unknowing even as we are known.

On this slab the frail, unclothed body was found;
blood and excrement sloped off the incised wounds;
shards of memento mori were strewn in the filth;
emblems stacked like identical black bags:
through the lighted window I watch the coming tide;
a solitary bather struggling amid shingles and foam;
the horizon's englobed splendour in total solitude.

Because murder is never given, everyone agrees
the flowing tide is impervious to memory;
a tide spent on the coming coastline finally home.
What matter if the private majesty of a life
goes unfinished; movement and memory are reservoirs
in glorious reunion, the pride and the refuse.
And what matter if the darkening journey
can neither command nor disclose the secret thread

left behind by the running tides in this room;
the fleeing crowds return to what is always desired,
the duty owed to the dead in their wooden boxes,
the bricks and frescoes iced-over and torched.
The bather clambers over mud and earth numb;
the mind's weight on ancient floors,
disabled by the uncleared and guttered mounds.

He approaches the threshold,
in his mind's wandering a terrestrial fire,
a possibility without impending, insecure,
free from pain and all hurt desire;
in his weightless sanctity tired and on edge,
passing the body hunched in the snow,
unknowing too of exergual form, imagining

the arc of blood *disdeining imploied dies*;
a vesture's comity in oyster-white shells;
ascending images of decayed perseity
like gulls coursing shallows of the will,
so *light and quick, coyned and plentiful,*
wheeling above enamelled seas;
moral failures ever vigilant for an *eafie* death.

Along the sea-edge patches of ice recede
as light moves across the ever-shining waters,
the passage of sun and stars equalling bled desire
and all original being amid passersby
cast out in the world's deeper darkness;
the evening sun on edges of swords and frozen rivers,
as fear and blood merge
in foul-smelling rooms on pale sofas.

That beneath these wounds tongues have issue,
and unworthy *bee* to the ripped ligaments;
there are no obstacles to border these obscurities
as sea weeds linger and drift in the sea:
Max, if these chancels and vaults are shields
do not pity me my rank consolation,
good is suborned to the milled edge,
attrition enough for the life of each victim.

And what matter if after the storm several trees were lost
bringing broad daylight into the middle of the room;
an equal advance of the bright exhalation
attends these things, repairs the luminous flood,
across fire and water, saw and scrim,
remnants of an improper death,
the revenants of rancour and malice now walled in
by embedded ironwork and voids on coastal paths.

When in these hours I am held by extent
by the shore, the low tides chancred along wharves,
the age of all that we are no more than joists;
in the salvaging there is much to be done—
strap and mace the flesh so others can join in
the end of the pier finally before me—Don't pity me, Max.

3

Max, from the rotting carcasses come new swarms,
a purity integral to surmise and warrant, and there
the bees remain conjugal to sealed estate.
For before honey these names are engaged
amid a coastline ceremony; a honeyed weal
for an offerer winnowed by excess;
the hives submerged by many infidelities;
by depths so profound we abide in fear.

I wander past traces of old water-mills, the soil
carries traces of weald and marsh, honeyed waters
for domainial claims beside milling ports;
against magister and icons, disused hand-querns,
my mind's density resonant with issues,
an obliquity of truly lovable being: these dues warranty
here, absorbent by sunlight through reflective cloud,
the light equable and implied, by a temperate life.

Beyond the limestone uplands live labourers,
solitary, silent, poor: in small fields
they circle each virgate passion, eat the seeds.
I met an old sailor there who sang memories
of the tide's enabling astride the open sea;
his call and rasp held the perfection and the doubting,
and all inward equality; shaking with the praises
on high moorland fields.

First honours are reserved to constancies
some epochal rigidity on the high watershed;
for here Cistercian stones disclose a destiny
on some inexcusable trespass, fiducial comity at the wetter edge—
where meridians and stars are roughly named: and I
watch the children playing in the unfrozen meadows near Rievaulx,
the pacing of completion and the auspices of trust;
how their oblate measures for the coming light,

and all the qualities resorted to as contraries,
shift the primacy; and how their voices sound equably
in the stellar heavens despite manorial hardship;
for on this land newly assarted within enclosures and acreage fees,
pity is interminable, unwieldy for common use,
a libration of good which apportions trust,
burning the small hands with light pressure
as they leave, undone, an edifice of love and games.

Honeycombed stores, therefore, are sole agency,
a chapelry wherein every solitary prospect
is, as it were, right compulsion, single arch,
inducing dismissal of opposite abysses, the keener poise;
for we mistake the discharge of arrears
for remoter visibility on bracken-dense moors:
and gently edge the mind's unfoldings in embayed forms.

That these gains are immodest, Max, without fealty,
pledged into being too high above reticence,
free from investiture, contrary belonging,
rubble markings across rolling ridges of open fields;
what seems conspires, the time of letting ends,
an old man's plaintive chant sings of lapping splendours,
the snow and winds against him and hard on the sails,
and life assembles many covenants you and I share.

And if I were to remain unsated, too passive
to attract complices to ease feelings of reprobacy,
I am not sure I could dissuade or distract
from the sea's intrusion flooding these fields:
neither the fasting nor the festival
can reclaim back lowland tide-water depositories,
nor recover the unfactorable arc of the heavens:
juridical assent demands solicitude for those who fail.

The bee-keeper loves all prosperous change;
and when the three distances are too great,
he can gorge without measure on the natural earth
where rescission, disabused in obliquity and harm,
becomes a honeyed psalm dropping sweetly through cloud,
an indebted circle all honey and blood, fish and birds.
The arisen flood is thus desperate recourse,
remoter for being among us the more.

I am so much fallen, Max, in the least of things least,
amidst these people privately knowing,
dismembered by intemperate skies,
I am like a bruised fruit left half-eaten,
mirrored in each part of the unmoved and permanent world
like charm upon the river, or a cardinal thought,
a hive of single words exchanging its dwelling place
for manifold—memory, itself, roof of the world.

The Chosen

The poverty of San Francisco—they say—is its karaoke—
the burned-out buildings burn in unison,
rioters sing with perfect pitch and intonation.
Dark news—they say—is elsewhere:
like the kissable, dark-lined foreheads of negroes

bent over paper cups, like the image in your eyes—
'illuminated by the greatest concentration of colour'.
Put on your red dress, baby-girl, there's a northeaster coming;
people cover us, as the broken freezer releases watery ice:
only to be dying of sadness coz the hamburger is cold.

From all outward appearances this world 'works'.
The heel has snapped, as ordered,
and you do not miss a chance to say how *good* the burger is;
that the lettuce, and spices, are an ideal of beauty;
that the onions are an archetype of the genus *burger*,

the bun faultless. But the waitress wants no part,
there is a price for sympathy, and your meanness is an art.
You and I and the model citizen
without avatars, but regnal in our emerging—
out of step because we have lost our concern

for the terror of the soul. It's a simple pendulum
that casts doubt on the pure colours of feeling—
perhaps all that is wanted is a world lost before time:
that evening when you gave raw fish to the Village People
saying it was a metaphor for the 'mens',

and the Chief said it was a wound that went deep.
'Give the boy rice,' heard from the fishing boats,
the sounds on the karaoke playing running water,
sea storms rising 'from above alone' onto the flats—
then a high degree of baffle as the flow of ice averages

many famous sounds; eating, as you know, a burger
lost in dreams of the sea and the profits made by chains.

The Wandering

'being yet to begin my first houres attendance'

On the grass banks beside the narrow estuary
in the close, well-fenced textures of night, where death
leads me without memories into the never coming nearer
and never going away, in the holy infalling darknesses
hoping to become hope in the being of what becomes,
farther and farther from myself in longing of the same,
I willingly call for the journeying rings
and join with the pierced ones in the becoming of the hurled.

Above me starlings wheel over wind and estuary
drawing closer still at my approach, seemingly dispossessed;
and yet, how dark the water is, how high the reeds;
lightning swirls in all the waters of the world,
for the time is deepening, and so too the bridges of the air, —
for nearer and truer now is the wing-tipped deafening
as I put on the weight of mutability
and my eyes become yielding seeds,
and I find myself a riven shell rivened deeper by the soaring birds.

That is a generated birth, amassed, rising into sight,
beating the air above the evening surf,
an ascension always beyond me, I never there.
Whether I have wandered from place to place,
and in my wandering, bathed in the depths of reflection
become the rush of water in rains;
you have been a beacon to me in my outward journeying,
a brimming gourd in the solace of the same,
until the farther shore is the anguish of nearness, a seed washed into rind.

Alone in my weariness death leads me far, the wide
desolate spaces teeming with the outcry of birds.
And in the dark difficult hours the world is englobed
by these selfsame birds wheeling above edifices of sight;
from their wandering I see my own disappearing mind
beyond the gorge and foreshore in the quickening light;
for in the tributaries of the heart the mind is riderless,
fulfilled in the wonder of dying and the dead of my breaking life.

For what am I, in my wandering, but a doubt and dark,
without diffidence in the internal fires, or my dark intentness,
so openly, it seems, I am like that dejected one
whose weal and sustenance drown in the waters of the sea,
the inquietude of murder greater within the flame?
What, given so much inner abuse, could I be but inaction,
a majestic reticence in face of the non-ordained?

All that there is, can and ought to be is suffering,
for longing is the agony of the luminosity of the distant,
and in speech a frozenness no name can endure
unclenched at the very root: and in the shaft-light solitudes,
burning into shallowness my own burnished reflection,
there is a desolation deep within my seeming,
unable to understand the hope and promise of the offering,
flung into being among the star-shaped altitudes.

For without the signs on the firmament and mountains
how will the circle will find itself? How will the animals
walk inquiringly into the open fields
and drink searchingly from the open wells?
What certainties must fall if we fall also,
holding our vigilance for landing on the headland
like sounds of remote resonance in the ear,
in the world-shell, trying to become it with our names?

Will the mind be truly be empowered with virtuality and will
as in that most exquisite occasion when the groundless
gave forth honey and names into the land of the dying,
and speech, ensured, gave forth longing and hope?
Surely there was serenity in *that* fall of fruit in the garden?
Now, when I am nothing but sadness, and sadness
breathes in my lungs, and sadness flows through my veins,
you come back to me and ease the sorrows of my heart.

How am I to know it, this surety of good,
to do all that is noble in fastnesses at evening,
when the eye is wearied by seeing and the ear is wearied by hearing,
and the appointed ransom of my end thunders into darkness,
uplifted by you from the frailty of the drowned?
Surely among the mind's partial flood is a returning world,
a moveless ark in the brilliancy of the unseen;
or do the outgoing streams seethe inside the origin,
darkening the rock-faults and rinds beneath the keel?

Now, as the horizon fades and stars flame over the shore,
and the darkened skies shine with exalted splendours,
and wing-tipped fires burden the concussed air,
burning the throat until I am mute with muteness,
death slices through my tongue and forehead
with a sword in whose tempering fire and water transcend themselves;
the ebbing tenderness marring both anvil and stone,
as the graces set free suffice a life cleaved asunder
become once again an unfolding flame.

At Chartres

Below the fields and pathways
& fifty-five-gallon drums
              on fire with deep blue flame,
I find myself caught wide-eyed & dumb
in the masses,
              trying very hard to be 'public'
but the people are sweating & my mouth hangs—
the tins are too heavy
              & the fish are strapped to my back—
people crowd round the fires to warm themselves
as if this were Lord Hideyoshi's Castle,
    the tour of its splendour
                    a mirror to the whole world:
    forced to pass along the *engawa*
        as black thunder strides across the level earth.

In the air around us
        a smell of incense from the temple.
I feel such elation—as if I were
walking though a snowy forest
                    from Mercia to Wales.
The soul is a border,
    the ten canons a massive war on earth,
as lightermen hold in the fastness
                singing roaring songs
as the reveille sounds over moving crowds
    of tourists:

Then the leaf fall of memory,
as medieval monks mix pain with pleasure
flogging each other on green back roads,
each serpent, the skeleton mask beneath each cheek,
else subtly
        shrouded and hooded as the breath in the ear
saying 'kiss me'
        as I lay in my cot in the cell
                chanting, praying, kneeling,
saying 'kill me or fuck me'
        in the frigid waves of air
in the halls and sanctuaries outside my room.

Reaching down to the lawless deeps
        the only refuge: Bernard's liegemen
passing over the ruins of the dead
                with their tongues,
washing themselves in leaching pools of excrement—
                the blush of rage and shame
        as the nailheads pierce the scrotum,
the quality of beauty locked in the *last words*,
  naming each pain on the toilet floor
                of lepers.
Steeped in the soul like a net in the sea,
the pure find bliss in the plague,—
as the bearer of virtues comes home to the columned hall
  sunlighted
        the recantation 'it will pierce your heart':

the greenness of the moment the years' natural life
      in exile
above the treetops, walled towns, parks and meadows:
saying 'let me in'
      as I suffer again the days and nights of that room,
      pressed hard by the toils of virtue:
the crowds modulated in accord
with the leaching ground or flow,
laughing and singing in the ticket lines
  waiting to see the blood of the rose
              at the altar.

To A Surer Fire

Now, as I return to what I was in the beginning,
without guile of the lasting nor sufficient reason,
it's true the night air offers love without appearance, and yet—
without doubting I know my life has come and gone,
and my art and friends finally revealed for what they are—
immaculate deceits long upon the inning.

Whether I have known and squandered, or fallen apart,
the prolonged predicates have neither assart nor fences
to front the heart's core:
the end that creates is a created world.
The guarded causes for which I once longed
(as changeless things, and not created) seem lustreless:

and all the beauty and speech categories in turn,
mottled by the rancorous centuries' intrusion
and all the bright eminence long upon the perning ground.

For changeless life continues in the justest world
and no quality resides in this, neither sword nor crozier:
the elemental fire more heat than light; as when
I stood on this curving ridge and recalled suffering things:
the boy choked and gagged and brutally forced
lost within the mercy of himself,
the temper of blood flowing from eyes and mouth;
blinded by fear and greater pain;
and the high places flooded with peripety.

How distant, now, the nave and aisles fronting the greens,
and the sea so far away, and the smell of lindens on upland hills—

memories of myself and the people I have loved,
without greenness in nature, or greening leaf to behold;
the just bridle of stars in shuddered hauls.

More keenly than you knew I swaddled each indignity,
even when the overhead stars drove me naked to the shore's cordage,
and I passed witless over the dark earth:
resigned in deferent and resistive memories
for you there was assent without prebend;
for me floodwaters and shale pouring into my soul.

Now loneliness laughs softly in my voice,
and the heart's meaning brims with obscurity,
delicious and dark like a northeaster blowing through the verge,
across the moist earth and open fields—
the falling world awash with water, warded above falling leaves:
startled by rapid cloud and leaching spill;
the breathless quiet carried, but apart from things.

I have often dreamed of such desolate sanctity
within the bare brightness of an unimagined world;
walking blindly in the dream's painful freshness
so as to return desolate and starred in what I already owe;
the first rules stranded in the vaulted folds,
and each renewal nobility or natural law;
all gone in the last hour to conformity of election,
or fresh watercourses in the valley below.

Yet I could not find the leal tangle of hope,
nor the watered heaths lying thick with stars—
for fear dispersed the brightest end—
and the broad charms of the dying a dying world;
the wet banks shining in the darkness, leaving
the infuriate life forgotten in the just minima of harm.

Out of the night and darkness of my own life's journey,
the low-browed candour of the proud
despite the timbered penury and moorland farm,
and the living stream reflecting all desired worlds:
it is pitiful to see human fires burning in the passing of the world,
as the lanes and streets pass out their lights,
and I burn from within like a jar full of ousted stars.

And still the great showers of rain pour down:
I am unable to endure the loss:
I would willingly give up the mired hoards,
and all the wayward fires,
just to be bereft of the apostasy— as for my art and friends,
may they have shame and nakedness and the lashing squalls.

For myself and the people that I have loved:
sheltering trees ragged above the tributaries,
and fining screes
edged and excrescent too swathe to hurt;
grief to enfold us— assort the cones of our vision:
mitred crowns of separating fire—
the freedom of being on rain-washed roads.

Tap

A sick and tired-looking Bill "Bojangles" Robinson dances lightly and quickly up the steps to the house. Shirley opens the door and invites him in. He sits down slowly, wearily, as if the act required great effort. She looks at him with a calm, almost malicious intensity, as indifferent to this show of weakness as to the bodily collapse it represents. Uncle Bo, her once-glorious edifice, no longer able to bear the load, as cameled now by her screen legend as a morning shadow by sunlight.

The room is unnaturally warm. The furniture and walls a uniform high pink. Shirley exits the room tap dancing only to return, a moment later, with a tray of drinks. She approaches Uncle Bo as if she were on a battlefield, dancing with all the grace and beauty given her, her ringlets flashing like a dying star, he the dark that surrounds it. He sits mute, mesmerized, with a measured smile, like Oedipus searching for his eyes in Gaza.

The colours are of fall,
the airports unvaried after the hotel lobbies & cafeterias,
and the jim crow cars I missed
      running barefoot in the dark,
  taking part of me away
as I led the line
      tapping quick steps on a table.

Footprints sparkle in the darkness.
The air thick with corn liquor,
the putrid mouths holler.
I passed through the swamp of white faces and burnt cork
  so footloose on the slats & hinges,
I slip-slid through the mud giddy, unhinged.
      It was a jig without a history.

Something deeper than skin
the whites sitting doubled over,
        their hands slapping their knees,
or coiling their arms into rope as my legs ran amok;
their blacked-up faces
    in shock as if I were a smear in the pigment,
or a limp trying to disguise itself in the firm thrusts.

Then came Shirley,
  rehearsing the shooting
    demanding the flash and bursts
      through the backstage era,
    onto the freeways riding through the night . . .

She covered my loins with dimples and laughter—
I couldn't get enough of the towns, cities, and theatres
or this rote version of myself clumsy, unable to stand.
            No touching, no danger. But even then,
    when we danced on unshattered legs,
            I felt a noose closing:
the weight of the past tap tapping on my crippled legs.

My dances were syllabaries:
hard-won movements whipping the air,
loose-limbed flings towards freedom,
        jigs blazing in the blood
    along the hips, knees, ankles, shoulders, and elbows,—
even when I played the darky I was never blackened.

Now when my soul trembles
under the moon,
in the light of my nighttime mind,
in the blur of form and memory,
nothing moves my body but gravity—
I mean, I arrive limping, my heart stumbles,
like a child who can't walk yet,
ready to carry all the weight of those years,
   about to leap, headlong, onto the stage,
      and stamp this arrhythmia out of my body . . .

The Block

The Block It is a work in bronze, pitched against the connivings of history. It is a memorial to the ditch and the improvised burial— thrown into the nigger pit after the flash and burst. And his father keening repeating the line that such burial was an honour. What perishes and lives, image to fit the sudden and violent end, when ending itself is history? He scrapes and scrapes, as a child might, for what has been left behind. He digs deeper than is necessary. A mist descends so opaque it blurs the horizon line where the blacks who frame him, men who cracked jokes as they readied for the firing, were lost to the smoke and fumes. Who now cares how? Think of them marching into another time frame, cut and edited, where bronze machine signs burn fleetingly at the wintry end of the world.

I recollect now that registry and that time. I act my part. So nigh is grandeur to our dust, so near the abyss of what remains. Let those who are scattered be reclaimed. The light is needed, it comes to where it is. I am not like those other men. I pass by the Lapis Niger, on my way south to where the fallen ones dwell. Now I remember. Now I remember it all.

The auction *The group of blacks seem frozen in time. As the auctioneer opens the bidding, time seems to flow backward, as if something reminding, as if something wanting to sound. It is a public square in North Carolina. The milling crowd, restless, press in with all the weight of ritual. Something passes telepathically between them, something in the sound of the auctioneer's voice, something in the assured inflection and pronunciation—words, that is, so close to hand they belie all forms of accusation. All—the blacks included—hear something painful and ever echoing as the bidding opens, something unreflective, essentially artless, as time begins to flow backward, into time past. There is the odd mingling of disinterested curiosity, even tenderness, as the bids begin to flow and ebb. All else oversounding: the body and the blood and the ancestral word.*

Somewhere in the mist men are screaming, and their screams allow him to shape their grief, scattered over the inner crest. The dark casts of bronze in piles around his knees. Let them tend to him now, with knowledge and command, this abstract and stiff-jointed and gasping man. Moving—marching—downward souls, how uncertain go the turns, singing in the ranks, waiting to be primed by the muzzles and the rust into a single mass of wildness. The ditch is nearer. See it and leave. If you stay too long, you'll be finned by the bursts. The consecration of bronze for each unrecorded name. The hills and ridges and framing fields—and the men of the Fifty-fourth black against the sun.

Cut

'The hollows of his torso had the flayed look of a saint as the blood welled and streamed freely into the firmament. Each cut was studied minutely before the downward arc made new incisions. Black with a sheen of crimson — insignia of a job well done, the pain unbearable to watch but deserved. Is this not just punishment for a nigga who dares to question my authority?'

It was the springtime of my youth, the pulling of corn time. It was five years gone. I exhausted myself. The best of the work I do, the worst, never good enough. I was middling in my mind whether to stay or go. Then the falling of the stars began . . . some animals and some folks froze to death. Emptiness and such a great darkness — did He create or was He created by it? It was an omen. I was gone two moons before the horses and dogs brought me back. They said I was wild, untamed, devilish. That I was lost to this world. For my part, I don't mind. My dreams, moving slowly, tell me I'm home. . . .

So Long William Senyanga

'nothing fits the body so well as fire'
'*fucka*,'
rasping from the melting face,—
    'Room 22, Wembley Hotel'
a taste of blood hanging in the air.

The butcher stands in the middle of the room
amid cleavers, blocks, eviscerated beasts:
    you wake up to his suffering world . . .
he carves you like others carve soap—
a cigarette burns on the dyed red earth.

As dawn breaks smoke drifts over the forest,
we soak our knives in salt water:
salmon leap over silver flakes of ice
    in lakes glowing with white fire—
remember how we harnessed them? Now that night is falling?

Think of those sails of fresh linen billowing
in the tall rooms. How we drank brewed tea.
The petrol is moist and warm on your bare feet.
It slides down your naked waist
        shiny with blood and vomit.
You are already blinded, in torment, coughing.

What is worst—the great rifts of pain or the thick
   black waves of desire? Life burns in the darkness . . .
Remember when we sat under willow trees,
and the animals got all mixed up in the mist.
You were awed by the sodium glow of streetlamps.
Now you are scared in your eyes. Your ribs stripped.

But then I was the weakest. 'Not to be in pain anymore . . . .'
Those sunny winter days and cold nights,
steering cattle over the black mountains. You got the shivers.
You said, 'I am the man who watches others suffer' —
but words only come when everything is over,
so sharp, so painful: what I remember haunts me.

I'm sitting up in bed, panicking about the burial.
        I dream about it. It's bearable, yet I cannot bear it.
Why am I responsible   [too late, too soon]
                for the weight of this enduring world.

The Binding

Soon after you left it got cold and rained,
and I heard a voice on the phone that was you.
On the 15th the sun, alive again above the fog,
peered through the window. The voice said: 'hello?'

I wish I'd taped it, but the weather is bad again —
the voice takes me back, briefly, to our first meeting:
the girl I was with had you mesmerized by her offshore eyes,
while I was in mourning for my childhood. Now I mourn yours.

Across the sepia estuary redshanks, mallard and teal,
and one isolate mongol boy, neither buried nor received,
crowd in the squalls whilst others stray lost,
exhausted in gathered cloud on the horizon.

Above the flooding waters and flooding rains,
this endless drifting in the steerage seems unkind
when winds skein the stars on the sea white and black,
and birdcalls wash in cauls strewn by nests and temperies.

The voice said, 'I cannot envy you this goldpoint' —
as if memory vanishes like a shadow
and holds there, homing shorewards on turning tides,
awed by the self-unseeing and its mourning deluge.

Neither life nor death, nor the eeriness of the living
can wipe the slate clean, reburden the unvoicing;
what thrives is neither living nor its tormented gratuity,
but the world occluded — an island voice talking.

And as we walk together, cold, bad tempered,
beseiged by rain by wind, the tide-edge
reveals a drowned body turning in the wash,
the body appears white but is a parody of black,
blacked in guttural tides glistening with salvage.

Wondering what to believe ; wondering, too,
how to reflect the sunlight piercing in its flood,
slanting through irised rain and hard cloud,
rather than the dead reticulate with forgiveness;
in your world and its mooring, Doug,
there is an oracle that feeds turning breath into wreckage.

The voice said, 'Do not blame yourself unduly'.
It is through sacrifice that a name is killed—
now that the infinite is the cry of distance,
and these beaches, estuaries, and falling leaves,
have deepened to the limitless what is in the dying.

Gravitating about it to this ground,
gelid flights teem white and black, grey and brown;
in whose salient air all our soliloquies meet,
are censored, and restored as constancies,
for much that lies dead in us the dead lie round in kindness.

Herons

At the water's edge, waiting. A boy runs, gasping for air, eager to stop the dizziness. He wants to shout out Geronimo; he wants to announce his own recklessness as he falls down, gasping. He hears the roar descend, so close it stops his blood. He feels the waves pass over him, lapping forward in time and travelling over his body as he lies there trembling. In his oyster mouth the gentlest sort of rockabye rhyme, a guttural sound snatched from word and image. He hears his father call his name; he hears his father's anger as he pants rhythmically. In his mouth no words but a wash of black anguish whose flood no father could withstand. As he glances down through the water he sees the dark surface coming to meet him. Night with its hope of an end is still; the ocean nothing but an echo that he thinks he hears. Now there is nothing. Far, far below him, unseen but soundlessly floating up, traces of an unfurling vision, black and slender and curved like a beak.

He wishes there were a higher swell so he could more easily keep up the hope that what he hears is more than the drifting shadow of an echo. The things that abandon us, he thinks, like the words we swallow—words like 'prosper' that eat at us from the inside, oozing out like the jellified gunk all over his mouth and tongue. The spoken and unsuspected words—'He won't be cured'—borne along by a current from which there is no hope of rescue. Nothing if not isolate, he has marooned himself. He is an island with room for one castaway.

He jerks his head up, gasping and squinting painfully at his father's retreating figure stumbling amid the herons as they weave and shy off at the water's edge. He knows that there will be no reprieve. For the first time he notices that he is not frightened. He sees nothing but his own shadow in the empty water, hears nothing but his own distress echoing out across an empty ocean.

Look at the sea. He has always seen it thus, fixed by the landscape of his own past. A moment breathless, inflooding, hushed by the winds and waves and the dark currents underneath.

Notebook of a Return

"from the sea
        shed
are all my old desires"

— Stephen Jonas

In Memory of Radio

'New Black Music is this: Find the self, then kill it'
AMIRI BARAKA

The Trane. — If all the world is full of sound
then why are my ears so empty? Why have
I lost that passionate pitch, that way of
throwing the voice, word by word, beyond
the tongue's confusion? How can I set a
measure to it, make it leap when the blow
or beat is missing? When Trane walked
through the snow, so low in spirit he
could only mouth a vague, muted clam-
our, what did he hear if not the music of
the quantum moving on the back of his
hands, coming down wet on his lashes?
A music that keeps the mouth full while
bitterly consuming one's substance; the
music of time and the life of matter . . .
the sound the aging body makes when
dizzy from bending down; the arthritic,
emphysemic sound one hears when
retired more or less from everything; the
sound the dying one hears when snow
sublimes the horizon . . . I mean, the
sound I heard when I woke up this morn-
ing into the world's possibility and off-key
changes echo in the bad air, the shadows
freeze on the wall, and my stiff-jointed
body flails . . . Imagine those changes ring-
ing still as the aging musician makes his
way through snow up to his knees,
nobody around to see or hear him falter-

ing. Can only blues poets hear him? Those changes rolling off the line and the hard rhythms orbiting around the moist dry lips, as he drives through the night? A heartbeat to rime 'om' with 'freedom', 'sun' with 'ascension'; a tapping foot as the last take reaches the man inside, his beauty and ours. The apotheosis as a hundred triumphs lets fall a thousand humiliations onto the floor of time. See him standing up wearily against the wall, his troubled body shaking with the vapours and flames as each note falls into ashes.

The Tenor. — And for those who understand black music as the third ear — figured out, unspoken — receiver of voice, spirit, nation: on the radio the dream is anguish in the air, a memory of the life lost to him now, as he turns away, on his hair flakes of blown snow, streaks of ashes . . .

Jazz music as echo, nothing but echo, a sound that, so the rumour went, struck him by its foreignness. And the woman whom he loved for all her stammering, the measure of each loss, irresistible, unyielding. Her suffering the tempo and the urging behind all of the pieces. To love someone and watch them die . . . the years mourned like a melody blowing softly in the ear. Would it be worse not to hear it?

Image

Midnight. A cab like any other.
John, Maudie, Vicky, and me:
waiting for the future to close in—
we've paid our tab and want something new
       the grave and layered absence at the end of night,
nightlights on the river.
It's romantic but we approach it without sadness
     or fear.

The great cold is closing in.
After the leftovers on each other's plates
       have become bags of garbage for drunks and vermin.
You know, it's funny, the four of us panting as we walk,
       gasping and panting as if we were in a movie.
a visible faith to embrace on the road
          as we ride headlong into the darkness.
Driven,
      (I keep replaying the future, in weaves and fragments)
        the trance lasts only a minute . . .
Maudie's blood, Vicky lacerated,
     And I see my own face pressed up against the glass
as if the duress of spirit hurries to keep up
     with the randomness of things,
       the newly enhanced focus on disaster
   a word
      a collision
         a memory of blood in the mouth—
the marks and scars as if we are out on an open sea
    a storm landing on the water,
       the silvery blue elation of forces

but no secondary pleasure of recall. Just the outmanoeuvred identity.
　　We can find it if we have to.

There is only one way home.
　　Maudie feels sick, Vicky is stoical, John is unharmed but guilty.
　See, time is moving backwards.
　　It mounts and spreads on the river.
　It pushes snow off the branches.
　　Its wave-form an oil stain on a napkin.
"That's everything connected," I said.
　　That's why we have to know this. Avoid manic cabs.
Or the following mis-cued sequence:
　　of one continuous shot
　showing four men hitting down
　　on some dark and shapeless thing, repeatedly,
a strange way to spend a morning
　　walking out of the past onto darkened roads . . .

Names of the Fathers

My shadow doused the light when the stars fell
black against a black daytime black again . . . and the light, the light
freezing into blocks of ice falling through pitch-black heaven
as the stars fell. What isolation
—wordless on the grief-blackened earth—
and why this monumental impossible light, black again?
And why has the blemished child returned to us?
And this parting though we absent mourn
a turning away from a fascination so dear to us?
And what will happen to the fathers who refuse to deny us?
what will happen to the stigma of the name?
A dream of the hearth
and then the lure of murder . . . forced to take the dead son's place.
Each child smiles warmly a radiant witness
as the last light edges into the darkness,
exiled before the mysterious cabin and sleep with no shadow,
killed repeatedly in an ecstasy of time.
There was no house in the woods and yet the father compelled us
and the two sisters played whats and why nots in the wintry darkness
mournfully unveiled.

Lying father, lying ghost—in whose name we speak.
We need the tomb of the murdered child
buried beneath ice and fallen snow,
we need the trauma that predates us
the issues and the summons,
weaned into the loving memory of death and of nothingness,
the sacred beginning of the book.
As we go out on to the black frozen lakes of night
murmuring remembering possessing
wanting to cry out in the dark
in whose name should we remember you?

What will happen to those anasemias
thresholds and old mystic grandmothers
born knowing Greta's secret in the long unlighted tunnel?
In this living memorial
will the long-memoried become an empty husk not to be passed on
like a daughter's remorse
amid news of the world's end and a black sun,
doomed to roam the stars in the company of the lost one? ...
As the last star fades into nothingness
we are born knowing
that in our father's house the lost one can't be forgiven ...
Exile is a story not not to be passed on ...
And Greta's secret is in heaven with her eyes and bones.

Notebook of a Return

'there are no rites
for those who have returned'

1

Lebensbahn—When I first saw it, waiting like some utopia or catastrophe on the edges of a dream, there by the edge of the sea, I was overcome. Having shed so much and abandoned what little known, I was no longer sure if I was dreaming or awake. In my mind it felt as if I were descending into a shadowed room, a breathless abyss— it daunted me, these ruins of glass and steel standing above the hissing traffic like doomed palaces of distraction. It feeds my inadequacy. It looms . . . the first tremors of awakening at the edge of my field of vision.

Clouds pass, heavy with rain. For a moment the canons also seem to be falling. For what is an event but a symbol and word for the future? A tide leading us into the great dark night?

Eurybates—History repeats itself. It is a question, always, of loss or shipwreck. For a long time we followed him: we stood but as a plank to his ship; he was the tide that, at its flood, would lead us on to fortune, that would take us home if we but learned to venture as and when his current served. Now we despise him, considering our lot. It almost forces us to grasp our freedom, bound in the shallows and miseries of being black men. At first, there was something artless and trusting in his wish to be another Marcus Garvey. The aura surrounding him was like a ravishing untimeliness, fixed like a moment in a dream, pointed like a letter of the alphabet. Now watching him pace the decks, I needs must ask: was he ever equal to the hardness of things? Did he offer us anything more than the amazement of a child?

On the edge of ground-zero halo'd by fallout, the silos and test ranges show white in each thermal burst. Like my first glimpse of the amphora, an edifice of shanked bone forms on the rim of the world, the ruin self-enclosed. I can't quite reach it—the horizon veils the dark, deserted earth. But exile is not a story to be passed on, only the chaos of water remains . . . "After the Negro was freed he was like a ship without a rudder". These letters name a fixed sequence; words cut from the history of the world. Words beyond words, deep, like an anchor chain. We know this— the signals weigh heavier as do the outcomes of war.

The blacks say silence will be our last witness as we sail into nothing. Not thunderstorms or tempests, but a sound of incompleteness strange and reawakening on the rim of the ear. The stars will stop, rigid, engulfed by the darkness. Erased

And the air slides towards the white flashes, the horizon pillared and grand as far as the eye can see. It is like being free again, even though the fires we cross bring us to the point of surrender . . .

My soul has grown deep by the vast oceans I have crossed even though, at first, I was loathe to make the pilgrimage. I didn't want to go because I didn't relish the idea of running a fool's errand. The omens were ominous, full of anxious beginnings. Then the winds stopped and silence reigned, and a charged rumble seemed a long time in defining itself as something besides a derangement of nature, some onrushing nameless event. I wanted, above all, to stay waterborne, sweeping from sea to raging

by the loneliness of time. Then the last charged moment as we watch from the decks ... the air will be full of the heavy gusts of words. A rain of Swahili or Greek, Russian or Yoruba. A phantasmal gleam, painful and ever echoing, as we veer into ground zero. "The world will end here," Eurybates says, "as we round the point of the dark broad seas." The vision came to him in the shape of a stunted human figure running at sunrise through a battlefield. His veil a gift, like an infant's caul, endowing him with second sight. It is, he says, his one meditative passion; a figure of difference drowning out the false voices we hear. It goes deep, this recognition: bounded in a nutshell, but ordering the vast bounds of space.

sea. Now time is totally lost to me having reached so long for so little. I don't remember it. Nothing sticks to me but the failure of having done. This is dead time. It never happened until it happens again. Then it never happened.

II

The boat heaves in the driving rain,
  I see myself fall into the depths
  alone, but also laughing.
Through the long night, too long, I wait for it:
Comrades, I am the lost one from a lost country.

On the bowsprit
        the old men sing mantras as dawn breaks—
it is the hour when Ethiopia rises and stretches forth,
    adrift in the cruel blue
        the day
the hour when nations rise near and far, waiting for the message.

The omegas and alphas
        waiting for the letters to name the end:
  the last guttural before the world ends,
as the triumph of a journey
                        outlasting time
  disappears under the waves of the sea.

Lashed to the mast
  as the prow turns to leeward,
        and light sinks into the maelstrom,
waiting for the roar to reach the rim of the ear,
        this event: it's too ample,
  I don't want to see the wolves come into their own.

The letters uttered will not save us:
  against my will the world is tossing me
      like a ship upon the sea:
    I got it writ on the tail of my shirt—
or maybe the coming wilderness is not the end

but what has ended: the who we are and will be.

III

The Alphabet. — When Odysseus invited us to share in the perils and glory of bringing Greek to Africa, I was one of the first to volunteer. I endured hunger and thirst, and all the hardships of war, because I wanted to track an alphabet through deserts and jungle. This was the summons and the duty: to make the speechless speak, to bend nature to the power of language; and so I starved myself rather than risk a word or a syllable. I could not wait to hear the first people's voices whose sounds, we believed, would come to us unexpectedly. Waiting for the journey to end took us weeks and months — the sun was very low when we saw them, veiled figures walking in the distance obscured by heat and by sand. We waited, eager to hear the riddles of their conversation. At first we couldn't figure out the accent. And then, light began to break somewhere as the syllables began to join into words, sprouting quickly into names.

"The word," he said, "can only be regarded as the pathway of doubt, or more precisely as the way of despair." "You can't mean that," I replied, careful not to sound accusatory, or hurtful. "I'm not sure what I mean," he said, rather testily. As we stood on deck watching the stars fall on the waters, I tried to think of something funny to say but, as the night fell, my voice fell away, my words heavy as though moving through an echo chamber. Then he turned to me. "Eurybates," he said, grabbing me roughly by the shoulder forcing me to look into his sad-eyed, leaden face. "You and I are both set apart from the world, we wander behind the languages and categories, you, immersed in your natural and innocent forgetfulness, and me, sounding through the remote edges of thought, sadder and lonelier even than pain or loss." This must be when history turns into fiction, or when a sense of day and the land becomes animal,

As we sat across the aisle listening to what we now knew to be veiled women, we realised we were hearing our own words mirrored. Our astonishment was total and so was our grief. We felt like mothers looking for letters they will never see, wives waiting for voices they will never hear, children listening for footfalls that will never come. I sat back, rigid, I opened my eyes and saw that the sky was black. I sat in the dust with my eyes open and I realised that the sun had gone from the sky. I looked up to see deep rivers of words, knotted and mazed, flow over the surfaces. An alphabet of utter chaos raining down on the clear-minded; in our open mouths letters and words gasping for the cries of our fathers. Odysseus began shouting in a rasping voice — the letters were a call to war, a cloud of ashes blood-borne. As the women repeated the letters, the shock made us squat like women on the ground, our arms wrapped around our knees. We began to think we didn't exist, erased. It mere nature, an echo roaring madly through the future to come. "I'm not sure what you mean," I replied, thinking all the while of the many differences between us, of how my life had been shaped by the open sewer of his ambition, the subsequent shame thereof, but also by the weight and fluidity of memory, its layers of dissolution, longing and emptiness. All I knew was that, all at once, after reaching so long for a star we had been plunged into chaos. Mine the loss and the steerage; his the discovery and the final gain.

The dark is all around us. He looks up at the words, drifting across the starry ceiling. We see miracles and visions intermittently through a dark mist. He swims out to them until he can no longer be seen. The eternal sadness fades as we set the boat on fire and begin to lash ourselves with sisal and hemp. The moment a monument to itself, naming the names with

seemed that words had no difference; the likeness a kind of death, an echo of experience. A figure then appeared out of the barrens, coiled like a viper in a pail, or a gorgon. We didn't say a word, mesmerised by the light flashing on its wings, the wash of honey-gold at the nape of its neck, and the curl of its black diamondlike talons. It was so nearly upon us, swooping down so squarely and vastly, it looked more like a swarm than a single thing. It was too big, too empty, for either word or vision. Then we all stood up at the same time. We looked up at it like semi-drowned men, and remembered what it was we had come to say. When we speak what remains is the word, and how, because of that, even the depths have a name, which is why the last wish of all is always the same: to live as if we will never die, and to love life as if it were already lost, for death too must be loved if life is to dwell in the name.

no one to ever hear them or know how to hear.

The Drowners

Terror is the truth of the world
And the sounds which linger on destruction are gathered
      in the dimming sky.
Was it my doing? This proud grief which laments each crime
while blackened corpses burst open like stars; in their fetid wake
the fire-hammered air of rivened stone
teeming the dark anvil, then lighting the stone
in billows of pale smoke massing a block away
with smoke iron its mentioning, till risen flare.
I ignored reflections of promise and error.
Across my own wild care, heads and torsos emerging,
the water was swirling, with the moon's tide.

Memories of torture and of war,
Like emergent fires underground: make these tourists burn
as bombed-out buses sit dead in traffic. Let every imploding window,
every fractured limb, strut the light surface of fire/stone
and smoothing this refine. Death honours those who do not seek it;
cutting the loose tendons and the frail neck:
the exploding limbs, the husk and breath with one surging pulse,
it measures qasidas for my love's command.
Though terminals never gate the ancestral tide
of this coming war beyond the blank wrath
of these arcing devices, I am joyous
if my belt gives comfort to one amputated limb.
Prime the trigger. More air to burn, heave,
than flocks of hot iron, firm sweltering play,
wing-tipped fires in the foundry's liquid heart,
from quick fall to taut still with mushrooming head,
and from this sacrifice, I incinerate every eye and ear,

the red flood on shore bordering on burial,
and the one grand murder rending limbs like stones
split to the ore's rawness; I have only one truth:

The hammer, the anvil, the wheeling, the ravening fury—
The bridge to a quiet province now looming out,
beyond coastlines fronting distance with shadow
and a burning colony, where beams of light
pound the days and hours. There are so many of us.
As many drowners as there are broken bodies
on that bleached shore from which life is taken
like broken branches on to the bonfire's height.
But life must fall, onto tides and pebbles,
from a first love hatching, then to a final mould;
fall, and are still, just as this storm is one
pardon on shorelines of immeasurable murders . . .
my first sound was grief. Now, the stones weep.
I hear thanks and hate. I sleep, then I eat,
heavy with the life of unscrupulous forests.
I concede memory to the oblivion of stars,
and call up to pale death, content to outlast.
Sometimes I feel just, and the eternal grief lifts
on the ship carrying its load and the moon's tidal
pull on waters, and the spell tightens round me
like a belt's tight border making me warm.
Martyrs sing out to me from the midst of their greed.

Photophonics

1

'Had everyone gone mad'

Bion at war. — They were passing strangers in the world. The world was a vast dream taking shape by itself, an event filling out — pouring out — from the centre of an idea. He noticed it but just couldn't figure it out. He could not disbelieve it or disrespect it, of course, especially if this was the way it had to happen, with all feelings mercenary, blasted by the true force of surveillance. The cold night air struck him sharply as he walked up the hill (he forgets which); the empty hollow feeling of not being there. This was something he remembered — the awfulness of living in the interstices. In this passage and movement he felt a sadness out of all proportion. But then everything was out of proportion. For one thing he discovered a new kind of aloneness, the event of peering inwardly but altering the outside world. The fascination of being detached from who he was, surrounded by night, trapped by the repulsive, and unashamed, glare of objects. They had so much radiance they made him feel unreservedly real. For the first and last

Behind the schematics of war in black and white he glimpsed the industry of vivid description. The noise of the cameras drowning out the interminable bombardments, the crack of machine-gun fire and rifle. War is lurking in the camera, already framed, awaiting the arrival of the fiery throng — the barrage — at the railhead. It shows him detraining tanks, unfurling maps, having recurring dreams. It is crude, blunt, relentless. It shows him waving a revolver at men running into the frame, only to be cut down by a child with a camera. It is the camera that puts him in the clearing — *dichtung* — hearing a mother's voice speak soothingly in German . . . Seeing someone at the moment he dies, phanta-

time, as the daylight of reason toppled into evening, a panic set in. His knowledge that he was real, thanks to a dark and encircling passion, at the limits of his vision, the way we all are now. sising the attack on screen, out there on the edges of perception men lost in the inferno of dust and fumes. It makes reality true, like the child involved in the work of schizophrenic dreaming. He had it coming, for letting himself be caught on camera. His obsessions, faint and faraway, engraved on the tape of a silent movie.

2

'I live like a man who's already dead'

MALCOLM X

L'image et son double.—I shall take one specific case. I am on my way to an uptown movie theatre. The trip takes me through strange neighbourhoods. Walking, I sense I'm being watched. Behind me I can see blood, my blood, marking the way I had come, collecting in puddles where I'd either stopped or lingered. I pass a knot of white men who stop speaking when they notice me, their eyes full of malevolence. I reach the house and go in down the rear stairwell. As I am shown to my seat all eyes are upon me. I wait, expectantly. A shadow begins to fall across the screen. My anxiety begins . . .

The Ligatures

was she speaking in your own name?

O Qui Perpetua . . . Tomorrow I'll disinter myself from my failed career. The time for ironic dialogue and tired supposition is over. Something like living needs to begin once again. Something I'm working out for myself, little by little. There's no need for the decline of my type, in vacuo, levelled by weakness, or fatalism. Still, it is hard to bridge the distances as we walk towards the white door, sign away all liability, deposit the cold harmless form, giddy with animal fear because death is no longer death, death is nothing.

When I first saw the newsreels I thought I'd suffocate — the echoes loomed over by something awesome. Take turns at the wheel, as the boat slips its moorings, be careful as we near midnight in icy winds: here the will is happy and natural, things remain aboard safe from the elements, the dead have not died, the corpses are not corpses. After all, hatred consumes us

Cartes à mémoire. — Heard but not audible; seen but not visible: a secretly heard distortion, remnant of a recontoured word. When the lights go out 'loss' is the true postscript. A few trains, subways, to remind us of the distance beneath our feet. It is impossible to share this since this moment is condensed from nothing, less than nothing; the rustle of the word 'mercy' when, standing in the yard, there is no better end than lying face down on the stones. Anyways, there's nothing to be gained — I write this out of irreverence, out of clear-eyed shame — the whole thing a vast desecration. And after the soapy skin and the approach to the half-open metal door — sure enough there is what feels like a fulfillment of law: neither just nor unjust, but simply a judgement as unaffected as the dusk by snow.

The equatorial star, now so familiar, can be seen through the windows, falling on the

precisely because we are consumptive, emaciated, starved of being alive. Sometimes, catastrophe is no more than the shame of having lived when the last one enters the going dark. It is a descensus and an aversion: the desecration that allows some to look while others turn away. For me to do today what is promised—to continue walking as the enemy approaches—there's something in my skin which rebels. I'm too emaciated—there's dust in my lungs, ash on my eyelashes.

manifold: here it is doll-like, veiled, as in an enigma, a reflecting shield whose abyss we witness. Where this is seen, there there is light, pure of all space be it of places or times, pure too of all conjecture of such a space. It follows, therefore, we are too deep an abyss, and needs must gaze through an ocean of gray shadow, too dim to see the world, too far away to lay hold of the unity above us and beyond us, every ready to hand.

The Angel knows I am not a Jew. He knows that the upper berth is empty. But knowing this does not purify fear, it just adds to the echo. But who is sleeping in the upper berth now, trailing limbs of immense coldness?

In Darkness

Heading west on alpine roads:
the light goes out, until we exit the Tunnel
open and clear-eyed, relieved and abashed
travelling between two fixed points.
Dark light as radio static pours out
and the afternoon play is only drivetime,
a speech in a play consisting entirely of what happens
because everything that happens happens to other people.
'Watch the road.' Avoid the bicycles.
The goddess on the highway ignites
on the high clear places near a lake.
And the car comes to rest on top of a dark light
with an afterimage of a very scared child.

We had driven here from Rome
the door ajar. (The rind, thrown windowward,
falls beneath the seats,
driving with dripping oranges
as the life talked about
is a shareable darkness nearly falling asleep.)

The scenery is of empty spaces or storms:
like a giddy childlike illusion, this is the next to last day.
The great northern vastness just an extended period. And in the middle
the half-dreamed vision and reproach
of nations and history closer to home.
The car drifts through clouds of compressed time: we arrive in rain
waiting for the long tense moment
as life slows down

finally after weeks barely slept,
the car moving along like a phantom of the road
for every passing minute there is, into the air of things.

Taking a road never seen before
wishing for the worst kind of pain
(knowing this to be the last act).
To the end of the road
'Tell me things you haven't told me,'
rounding the bend onto the narrow stepped street,
then to a bar and some beer and a mind emptied out.
Lost to everything but the journey.

Falling Snow

Trying to figure out
what message I should write,
watching the sun sink into the soulful dusk,
and snow falling on the Avenue. The security
of having a mask packed, this one
newly purchased. But the lone protester
keeps on collapsing under the police dogs.
The couple sitting on the park bench (so deep
in thoughts of sadness) nodded yes
as we traipse across the frozen grass
reading poetry aloud with seven kinds of irony,
word by word to avoid boredom and the war
of spirit because the whole sense of speaking
is itself a form of death. "Makes good copy,"
he says, "please write it down." A cab drifts by
and speeds away for maximum nigga-nohow effect.

Printed in the United Kingdom
by Lightning Source UK Ltd.
111829UKS00001B/64-111

9 781844 712618